UNLOCKING DELAYED BLESSINGS

By

Anthony Esenwa

© 2013 Anthony Esenwa. All right reserved.

First paper edition printed 2013 in the United States.

ISBN 978-0-9576469-0-2

No part of this book shall be reproduced or transmitted in any means, electronic or mechanical, including photocopying recording, or by any information retrieval system without written permission of the publisher.
Excerpts and quotes however, may be used without permission in magazines, articles, reviews, etc.

Bible texts from the New International Version unless otherwise stated.

Cover image by www.zedphoto.com

Published by Sichys Publishing.
info@sichyspublishing.com
www.sichyspublishing.com

Contents

Dedication 4
Introduction 5
God's Promises 7
What Has God Promised Us? 17
Who Can Claim God's Promises 25
Why Promises Look Unfulfilled 33
Take Your Blessings 44

Dedication

All Glory to the Almighty and Eternal God.

This book is dedicated to all who are still looking for the manifestation of God's promises in their lives.

Introduction

God is not human, that he should lie, not a human being, that he should change his mind. Does he speak and then not act? Does he promise and not fulfil? (Number 23:19)

Our God is immutable. Whatever he says He does. All his promises He fulfils. The bible is full of powerful and wonderful promises that God made to individuals and nations. We can draw on some of these promises by faith into our lives and receive the blessings in them. When God promised to bless Abraham he extended it to his descendants for ever and we are Abraham's descendants if we believe. The bible says that Christ has redeemed us from the curse of the law and transferred us into the blessings of Abraham whom God blessed in all things. The bible also tells us that as Isaac so are we children of promise which means that every blessing to our father Abraham can be extended to us as seeds of Abraham. If this is the case then how do we receive those promises?

There may also be private revelations that we receive directly from God or prophecies which we want God to fulfil so that they do not remain spiritual experiences only but potent influences in our lives in other for us to enjoy good quality lives.

My prayer is that all who read this book will encounter the needed light that will enable them draw from the power of God's promises which is able to change any situation positively to the glory of God. Amen

Anthony Esenwa
30th April, 2013

1

God's Promises

So the LORD gave Israel all the land he had sworn to give their forefathers, and they took possession of it and settled there. Not one of all the LORD's good promises to the house of Israel failed; everyone was fulfilled. (Joshua 21:43 & 45)

You can get every blessing you desire if you can find it in the word of God. God will do what he has said he will do. God has given us everything we need for a good and godly life but many times we can only receive them through our knowledge of him and what he has promised. If you know what God has promised concerning your situation you are one step towards unlocking his blessings for that situation. It is therefore very important to know what God has promised concerning your life and the particular blessings you desire.

What is a promise?
A promise is a pledge or a binding declaration to do or not to do something. While a promise can be made to one's self, it is usually made by one to another. A promise gives the right, to the one promised, to expect or claim the fulfilment of the specified act.

A promise can also be seen as an oath or word. We hear people say "I give you my word," when they make a promise.

When God gives us a promise He gives us His Word, and God's word can never fail. He said *"Heaven and earth will pass away, but my words will never pass away."* (Matthew 24:35)

The Bible is full of promises and has in fact been called a book of promises. We may read of prophecies and promises of God in the bible often and get so familiar with them that they lose their power and value.

The books of the bible, from Genesis to Revelations, recount God's promises to His people and how they were fulfilled. There are promises of inheritances, of victories, of rulership and dominion. We may sometimes ask; does God really mean those words literally or are they for special people?

Sometimes we may ask 'when will God's promises ever come to pass?' Some people may even begin to doubt the promises; doubting God's ability to do what he has promised. Sometimes when the Lord speaks and we wait a while for the fulfilment of his word, and nothing happens we question whether those who gave the message heard from God or if God even speaks at all to anybody.

God still speaks today and God keeps his promises. In many particular cases, however, many people do not know how to take their blessings and enjoy the fulfilled promise. We learn from scriptures that many who were blessed actually had to take the blessings in order to enjoy them. We have a lot of examples from the bible of how the fulfilment of some promises was received.

God's Promise To Abraham
God promised to make Abraham a great nation in Genesis 12:2.

> *And I will make of you a great nation, and I will bless you, and make your name great, so that you will be a blessing.* (Genesis 12:2)

At the time God told Abraham that he will become the father of a great nation he did not have a child, he was 75years old and his wife was barren (Genesis 12:4). It seemed impossible that the promise will be fulfilled.

Abraham waited for nearly twenty years before he got a child through his wife's maid (Genesis 16:3-16) and even then, God told him that the promised descendants will not come through Ismael, the child he got through Hagar, his wife's maid, but through a child he will have by his wife, Sarah.

The Lord repeated this promise to Abraham in Genesis 18:10, when he was nearly 100 years old and his wife was above 90years old. In fact on that occasion when Sarah overheard the promise that she will have a child she laughed and said *'After I have grown old, and my husband is old, shall I have pleasure?'* (Genesis 18:12). It was now probably over 20 years since Abraham first told her that God had promised them a child. She had become used to hearing it; in fact she had heard it so much it now sounded like a joke. It can be like that for us at times as well; we hear of the same prophecies again and again and we think 'they are just trying to make me feel happy'.

In the case of Abraham we know that God did fulfil His promise. God gave Abraham and his wife, Sarah, a child. Abraham was 100years old when the promise of Isaac was fulfilled; it took 25 years but the promise was fulfilled. At the time Sarah was long past her time of child bearing and Abraham's body was as good as dead. The bible tells us that;

> *Against all hope, Abraham in hope believed and so became the father of many nations, just as it had been said to him, "So shall your offspring be. Without weakening in his faith, he faced the fact that his body was as good as dead—since he was about a hundred years old—and that Sarah's womb was also dead. (Romans 4:18-19)*

Abraham believed and held fast unto his faith and he received what was promised. He was *'fully persuaded that God had power to do what he had promised.'* (Romans 4:21)

By this Abraham demonstrated his belief that God is not and cannot be limited by natural or logical circumstances. He believed in the God *'who gives life to the dead and calls into existence the things that do not exist.'* (Romans 4:17 ESV)

There are many other promises in the bible that looked impossible but God fulfilled them.

Israel And The Promise Land

Long before Jacob and his sons went to Egypt God had promised Abraham that He will bring them back to the land he promised him and his descendants.

> *Then the LORD said to him, "Know for certain that your descendants will be strangers in a country not their own, and they will be enslaved and mistreated four hundred years. But I will punish the nation they serve as slaves, and afterward they will come out with great possessions.* (Gen 15:13-14)

Many years after, the Israelites told this promise to their children, generation after generation. They lived in hope of the fulfilment of this promise for over four hundred years.

It is important to note that the promise land did not remain empty all the while that they were in Egypt waiting for the fulfilment of this promise. Other nations settled on the promise land and it looked a forgotten issue. It was difficulty to see how the promise was to be fulfilled – how other nations will be removed from the land for them to possess the land.

There are times when we think of the promises of God to us as gone beyond redemption; when we think that circumstances have changed and the promise can no longer be fulfilled; we think that the conditions which could have led to their fulfilment do not exist and cannot exist now, and we even try to tell God that we understand why He *'can no longer fulfil'* His promise in the given circumstance. We often forget, or may be, are ignorant of the fact that God actually does give *'life to the dead and calls into existence the things that do not exist.'* (Romans 4:17).

It was difficult to see how the nation of Israel was going to displace all the nations and tribes that had settled on the promise land before them. And some of these nations were well organised and powerful.
The ways of God are not the ways of man. When God decides to fulfil His promise, He does it irrespective of the circumstances.

> *For my thoughts are not your thoughts, neither are your ways my ways," declares the Lord. "As the heavens are higher than the earth, so are my ways higher than your ways and my thoughts than your thoughts.* (Isaiah 55:8-9)

Before God makes a promise He knows what will be the future situation or circumstance. God knew that by the time He will be giving Israel the promise land there will be many strong and powerful nations there, and that they will try to make the promise of no effect so He also provided for that in the big plan. We need to see God's promises from that point of view.

God is not too weak to fulfil His promise. He is not man that he should lie or change his mind. We have to, like Abraham, believe that God has power to do what he has promised to do.

At the appointed time in the life of the Israelites, God called Moses to lead them out of Egypt (Exodus 3: 1-11). Moses led Israel out of Egypt and through the desert by the hand of the God whose word cannot be broken. Joshua then continued to lead them into the promise land.

It is interesting to read at the end of Joshua's life in Joshua 21:43-45

> *So the LORD gave Israel ALL THE LAND he had sworn to give their forefathers, and they took possession of it and settled there. The LORD gave them rest on every side, just as he had sworn to their forefathers. Not one of their enemies withstood them; the LORD handed all their enemies over to them. Not one of all the LORD's good promises to the house of Israel failed; everyone was fulfilled.*

God fulfilled His promise and gave Israel rest just as He promised. He handed all their enemies to them and *not one* of their enemies withstood them.

It is very encouraging to read that God actually kept his promise to the Israelites. If he kept His word to them, He will keep His word to us because he said '*I the Lord do not change*' (Malachi 3:6).

We read of promises and prophecies in many parts of the bible, but it is so easy to overlook scriptures that states that God then fulfilled his promise with the detailed and clear expression as in Joshua 21:43-45.

2

What Has God Promised Us?

His divine power has given us everything we need for a godly life through our knowledge of him who called us by his own glory and goodness. Through these he has given us his very great and precious promises, so that through them you may participate in the divine nature, having escaped the corruption in the world caused by evil desires (2 Peter 1:3-4).

God has given us His great and precious promises, to enable us share in the divine nature, which is God's kind of life.

The scripture above is one amazing bumper-pack of life transforming treasures. An understanding of these two verses through the power of the Holy Spirit can turn any individual's life around for ever. The promises in those verses (2Peter 1:3-4) can be applied to every single challenge of life, from marital issues to bareness and unproductivity, perfect health, divine favours, prosperity and success in every single area of a person's life.

Consider verse four again, it says;

> *Through these he has given us his very great and precious promises, so that through them you may participate in the divine nature...* (2Peter 1:4)

A share in the divine nature is all that you need to overcome all the obstacles of life. It is a share in the very life of God. This is not just a spiritual life because we know that although God is Spirit He created the material world. So having a share of the divine nature can have a profound influence on the quality of our lives.

The perfect example of sharing in the divine nature in a material world is the life Jesus Christ lived while He was on earth; a life in which challenges just disappear when He came to the scene. Just like Jesus turned water into wine, and saved a wedding couple and their guests from shame and embarrassment, you come into anywhere there is a challenge and people say "Oh! Thank God this man (or this woman) came." Or you visit a family mourning the death of a young person, and like Jesus and Peter, you call the dead back to life. Or you come to a place where people are hungry and all of a sudden everybody is so filled there is left over. Or like Jesus sent Peter to get money from the mouth of a fish, you just solve financial problems with ease. That is divine nature – the nature of God, the nature of creativity and supplies. This is the kind of life God has promised to let us share in.

God has also promised divine health to those who obey and serve Him;

None will miscarry or be barren in your land. I will give you a full life span. (Exodus 23:26).

Also,

> *No one living in Zion will say, "I am ill"; and the sins of those who dwell there will be forgiven.* (Isaiah 33:24)

He has also promised us healing. In Jeremiah 30:17 the bible tells us

> *But I will restore you to health and heal your wounds, declares the LORD,*

God has also promised us success in business, career and all areas of our lives. The bible says in Deuteronomy 28:8;

> *The LORD will send a blessing on your barns and on everything you put your hand to. The LORD your God will bless you in the land he is giving you.*

In addition to these blessing we read in Galatians 3:13-14 that Christ, through His death, has given us access to the blessings of Abraham whom God blessed in all things.

God's Greatest Promise.

The greatest promises I believe God has given us is the promise of *HIMSELF*, "*I will be with you*". God has given us promises about various areas of our lives but to crown it all He also promised us Himself. This promise appears many times in different places to different people in both the Old and New Testaments. We also see this promise in some places as "*I will never leave you nor forsake you*".

In Genesis 28:15 we see God make that promise to Jacob;

> *I am with you and will watch over you wherever you go, and I will bring you back to this land. I will not leave you until I have done what I have promised you.*

The Lord also said to Joshua, after the death of Moses the servant of God;

> *No one will be able to stand against you all the days of your life. As I was with Moses, so I will be with you; I will never leave you nor forsake you.* (Joshua 1:5)

We know that God kept this promise to Joshua because for as long as Joshua led the people of Israel, not one of their enemies withstood them. The bible tells us in Joshua 21:44 that;

> *Not one of their enemies withstood them; the LORD gave all their enemies into their hands.*

In the New Testament we see Jesus repeat this promise and even goes further to expand it. In Matthew 28:20 He said;

And surely I am with you always, to the very end of the age.

In John 14:18 Jesus said to His disciples;

I will not leave you as orphans; I will come to you.

Before that verse Jesus had said in verses 16 and 17 that;

And I will ask the Father, and he will give you another advocate to help you and be with you forever— the Spirit of truth. The world cannot accept him, because it neither sees him nor knows him. But you know him, for he lives with you and will be in you (John 14:16-17)

Here Jesus promised the Holy Spirit which is the Spirit of the Father. Jesus also said I and the Father are one (John 10:30). So the Holy Spirit is also the Spirit of Jesus.

The presence of God through the Holy Spirit is the most important thing any person will ever need in life.

Jesus said; He will guide you into all truth (John 16:13). All truth means ALL TRUTH. It means all the truth about all the questions you will ever ask. He will lead you into all the truth about your life – your personal life and your relational life; all the truth about your health; all the truth about your marriage; all the truth about your ministry. He will simply unlock all answers to you.

The presence of the Holy Spirit can be likened to befriending someone who has the master key to all the doors you will ever need to go through. Some doors will never open no matter how hard you knock on them, if you do not have the key you will be wasting your time and energy. Some situations in life can be like those doors; you may cry and shout and moan or beg or try to seek favour they will not open if you do not have the keys or know the right thing to do. It is at times like these that you need the Holy Spirit and "He will guide you into all truth"

The Holy Spirit is God's best promise to us. The promise of Jesus, the Son of God, for the salvation of the world is already fulfilled. The bible tells us that;

when the right time came, God sent his Son, born of a woman, subject to the law. God sent him to buy freedom for us who were slaves to the law, so that he could adopt us as his very own children (Galatians 4:4-5)

The promise of redemption through our Lord Jesus Christ has been fulfilled. Christ has died, Christ is risen and He is now seated at the right hand of the Father.

The promise of the Holy Spirit is different. It is currently in effect and is one that every individual can claim into their personal life. This promise is still available for anyone who is born again. The bible say;

*And **afterward**, I will pour out my Spirit on all people. Your sons and daughters will prophesy, your old men will dream dreams, your young men will see visions. Even on my servants, both men and women, I will pour out my Spirit in those days.* (Joel 2:28-29)

'Afterwards' here means '*in the last days*' according to the Act 2:17. And we know that we live in the last days. So, lay hold on that promise and make it yours.

3

Who Can Claim God's Promises

Do not be afraid, little flock, for your Father has been pleased to give you the kingdom. (Luke 12:32)

Most things in life are given on the basis of criteria. Children are given gifts or inheritance from their parents because of the reason of being children. We may be given things by friends, parents or relatives because of the relationship we have them. Stranger are also given things or certain privileges or treated in certain ways because they are strangers.

God's promises are not just given to anybody and everybody. People have to qualify in some way to receive anything from God. God has laws about how His world and resources are managed and Himself is bound by His laws because His laws are perfect.

Jesus said in the book of Matthew;

Do not give dogs what is sacred; do not throw your pearls to pigs. (Matthew 7:6)

How Do You Qualify

Very truly I tell you, no one can see the kingdom of God unless they are born again. (John 3:3)

The kingdom of God means the domain where God is king; where God rules. The life of Jesus is a perfect example of the Kingdom of God. In His life we see the reign of God. The Acts of the Apostles tells us in chapter ten and verse thirty-eight that *Jesus went about doing good and healing all that were oppressed of the devil; for God was with Him.'*

All the signs and wonders that Jesus did were possible because God was with Him. He lived constantly in the kingdom of God. He told the Apostles that they were not of the world (John 15:19), which means that he was always conscious of the fact that he was not of the world although he lived in the world. Living the life of the kingdom of God will supernaturally unlock all delayed blessings.

God does not live with sinners for what has light to do with darkness. What is born of flesh is flesh, and the flesh cannot please God. Anyone who is not born again or received Jesus as Lord and Master is still flesh. You must be born again to live God's kind of life.

> *Yet to all who did receive him, to those who believed in his name, he gave the right to become children of God* (John1:12)

If you are not a child of God you are not of the family of God and cannot claim God's promise to His children.

Some received Jesus once and then turned away, and returned to the state where their father is the devil, the father of the wicked. They forfeit their right to claim God's promise because they no longer belong to God's family and cannot claim His promises. Sin separates us from God.

> *Surely the arm of the Lord is not too short to save, nor his ear too dull to hear. But your iniquities have separated you from your God. (Isaiah 59:1)*

People may come to church and mingle with Christian and even read the bible, pray and sing, but if deep in their heart they have not accepted the Lordship of Jesus and received Him they are not members of Christ's Body and cannot claim the promises of God. They may sometimes get some blessings as others are being blessed but they cannot claim or demand the blessings themselves because they are strangers and not citizens. They will only get the crumbs from the table because they are hanging around the banquet table, but the bread is for the children and not for dogs (Matthew 15:26-27).

How do You Become a Born Again

Nicodemus asked Jesus *"How can someone be born when they are old? Surely they cannot enter a second time into their mother's womb to be born!"* (John 3:4). And Jesus answered *"Very truly I tell you, no one can enter the kingdom of God unless they are born of water and the Spirit. Flesh gives birth to flesh, but the Spirit gives birth to spirit.* (John 3: 5-6)

A close study of John 3:1-8 and others parts of the bible we see that there are three main steps to be born again;
   1. You have to DECIDE to be born again;
   2. You have to be born of WATER;
   3. You have to be born of the SPIRIT.

If you are not already born again you can take that first step now. You have to decide to be born into God's family and become a child of God. God will not force you against your will. It is in your power to make that decision.

Being born again gives you access to the blessings you desire now and enables you to live God's kind of life. It preserves you here on earth and gives you eternal life with God in His Kingdom.

If you decide to give your life to Jesus and become a member of God's family or if you once belonged but went back to the world and want to reconnect to Him so that you can have a claim to His promises, then please make this prayer.

This is a prayer not just a part of this book. Pray these words;

A Prayer of dedication to God.
Father, I repent of all my sins because they offend you. Have mercy on me and wash me in the blood of Jesus your Son that was shed for my redemption. I receive Jesus into my life as Lord and Master. I dedicate my life to you and ask that you give me the grace to live your kind of life, in Jesus name I pray. Thank you, Lord, for your mercy. Amen

If you have consciously taken that step and made that prayer from your heart, Praise the Lord! You are born again. Heaven is rejoicing over you now. Congratulations on taking this major step. Haven taken this step, you have also partly taken the other step of being born by the Spirit.

Once you become a child of God, you are born of the Spirit of God who begins to bear witness with your spirit that you are a child of God. You have to foster this relationship by the power of that same Spirit. The Holy Spirit, will guide you and empower you. If you are not already a member of a bible believing church, then you have to join one. You cannot run the race of salvation alone. No one lives in a vacuum. You need support.

The other step is that you must be born of water; you must be baptised in water. Water baptism is a physical sign of the decision and resolve to be a child of God.

You, The Redeemed, Can Claim God's Promises
Being born again makes you supernatural. That which is born of flesh is flesh and what is born of the Spirit is spirit. You have access to turn the keys of life because your Father has willingly given it to you.

Every born again Christian belongs to Christ and God's family. It is through Christ that we have access to God (Eph. 2: 12) and become entitled to all the blessings of the children of God and the covenant of promise.

For through him we both have access to the Father by one Spirit. Consequently, you are no longer foreigners and strangers, but fellow citizens with God's people and also members of his household. (Ephesians 2:18–19)

We have access to covenant of promise through the blood of Jesus not by any personal achievement. You do not become entitled to your family inheritance by hearing of it. It becomes yours because you belong to the family.

As children of God through Christ, we are entitled to blessings through the redemptive work of Christ. Not because we earn them or deserve them but because Jesus Christ purchased them for us with His Blood.

He redeemed us in order that the blessing given to Abraham might come to the Gentiles through Christ Jesus, so that by faith we might receive the promise of the Spirit. (Galatians 3:14)

One word that is very important in our claiming a bible promise is *'entitled'*. If you are not entitled to God's blessings then you can only wait for the 'crumbs' to fall from the children's table, but if you become entitled through the redemptive work of Jesus Christ, then the blessings are yours for the asking. Then also can scriptures like this apply to you which says;

> *And I will do whatever you ask in my name, so that the Father may be glorified in the Son. You may ask me for anything in my name, and I will do it.* (John 14:13-14)

4

Why Promises Look Unfulfilled.

God is not human, that he should lie, not a human being, that he should change his mind. Does he speak and then not act? Does he promise and not fulfil? (Number 23:19)

God's promises can sometimes look unfulfilled, even when they have been fulfilled. God can bring us into our promise, or a place of blessing, and we still live as though nothing has changed, and sometimes we can actually give the blessings away.

There are times when God fulfils promises by His singular act; for example, if God promises rain, He will send rain. The beneficiaries of such blessings just pray and wait for their manifestation.

In many cases, however, the fulfilment of God's promises usually has two parts to it;

1. God's part and
2. Our part.

God's Part in The Fulfilment of A Promise.
This is where the Omnipotent God does what He promised to do for us to receive a blessing or the fulfilment of a promise. This happens in the supernatural. God commands the order of things to make room for breakthroughs for His Children. He prepares the grounds and brings us opportunities; He puts us in a favourable position to take our blessings and He expects us to take them.

God created all things and also calls into existence those things that are not (Romans 4:17). He is able to alter, and does alter, the order of things to give us a miracle. He parted the Red Sea for a whole nation to cross as if on dry land and fed them with food from heaven for forty years. He made the sun stand still in the middle of the sky for a full day for Joshua (Joshua 10:13). God withheld rain and dew for three years at the command of Elijah (1King 17 and 18). There are many instances in the bible where God changed the order of things for the sake of His children. He did them before and can do them again.

We hear of testimonies of miraculous healings and supernatural restorations and deliverances of people in many places, not just in bible times but today, all of them point to the fact that God is still changing the order of things to bless His people today.

> *He who did not spare his own Son, but gave him up for us all—how will he not also, along with him, graciously give us all things?* (Romans 8: 32)

God always does his part and expects us to do our part.

Our Part In The Fulfilment Of God's Promise

When Jesus fed the five thousand he took the five loaves and two fish and gave thanks to God and then he gave them to the disciples, and the disciples gave them to the people. The loaves and fish did not multiply before they were given to the people and would probably remain five loaves and two fish if the disciples refused to distribute them. Jesus who is one with the Father did his part and the disciples had to do their part.

The feeding of the five thousand is comparable to the first miracle at Cana in Galilee. This miracle of changing water to wine embodies what I believe should be the four main parts of an effective prayer;

1. Asking in faith,
2. Listening for God's instructions
3. Obeying God's instructions
4. Receiving the miracle

At the wedding at Cana, Mary went to Jesus and told him '*they have no wine*' (John 2:3). She was not just informing Jesus of the situation, she was making a request, and she expected him to do something. We know this because after speaking to Jesus she went to the servants and told them; '*do whatever he tells you*' (John 2:5). She probably knew Jesus was going to tell them to do something odd or strange, and he did. He told them to fill jars with water and then to draw from the jars to the master of the occasion. They obeyed Jesus' instructions and water was turned into wine. The master of the occasion, on tasting this new wine, said it was better than the first.

If the servants had not obeyed, there will be no wine and if they only obeyed the first instruction of filling the jars with water and argued that they wanted to see the water turned to wine before serving it to the master of the occasion there probably, will still be no wine.

So in that example we have this process; Mary made a request of Jesus, the servants heard the instructions, obeyed the instructions and a miracle was birthed.

In the second book of Chronicles in chapter twenty, a vast army came to make war against Judah when Jehoshaphat was king, he gathered the whole nation and they prayed and the word of God came to the king;

> *Do not be afraid or discouraged because of this vast army. For the battle is not yours, but God's. Tomorrow march down against them. They will be climbing up by the Pass of Ziz, and you will find them at the end of the gorge in the Desert of Jeruel. You will not have to fight this battle. Take up your positions; stand firm and see the deliverance*

the Lord will give you, O Judah and Jerusalem. Do not be afraid; do not be discouraged. Go out to face them tomorrow, and the Lord will be with you. (2 Chronicles 20:15-17)

Even in this case in which God said the '*battle is not yours...* 'Jehoshaphat and the army of Judah still had to do something they still had to '*go out to face them*' (2 Chronicles 20:17).

Taking a bold step in faith after we have prayed is an expression of our trust and belief in the power of God to act on our behalf.

Entering the Promise Land

On their journey to the Promise Land, God told the Israelites that when they enter that land to possess it, they should drive out all the nations living there and make no treaty with them (Deuteronomy 7:1-6). He promised to defeat those nations as they advanced.

and when the Lord your God has delivered them over to you and you have defeated them, then you must destroy them totally. Make no treaty with them, and show them no mercy. Do not intermarry with them. Do not give your daughters to their sons or take their daughters for your sons, for they will turn your sons away from following me to serve other gods, and the Lord's anger will burn against you and will quickly destroy you. (Deuteronomy 7:2-4).

After God gave them the land, however, they allowed some nations to continue to live with them. They did not drive them out but made them serve as slaves. Those nations became a snare to them later, but this is not God's fault.

Many times, God blesses us or fulfils a promise and we continue to live like the people of the world; we want to 'eat our cake and have it'. God does not give special blessings to a person just because he is human, although he can; He gives special blessings to his people. If God gives you a blessing or a miracle because you are His child then you have to continue to live as a child of God to enjoy that blessing.

Jesus makes it clear to us that there is a difference between God's people and those of the world. He said;

> *...you do not belong to the world, but I have chosen you out of the world.* (John 15:19)

It was up to Israel to move forward and take over the land as the Lord defeated their enemies. They were to take full possession. God had done His part; the enemy were afraid and scattered, they were discouraged and their strength had been broken. The land was there already conquered by God and ready to be taken. The inhabitants of the land were all afraid of Israel even before Israel came to them. Rahab told the spies that were sent to spy out Jericho that;

> *I know that the LORD has given you the land, and that the fear of you has fallen upon us, and that all the inhabitants of the land melt away before you* (Joshua 2:9).

This was before they actually attacked the city. God had discouraged them and made them afraid even before Israel got to them. It was up to Israel to take over.

God's part had been done. He had brought them to the land and afflicted their enemy with fear, theirs was just to drive out the enemy and take the land but they let some of their enemies live with them.

God had told them in Deuteronomy 7:22 that;

> *The LORD your God will clear away these nations before you **little by little**; you may not make an end of them at once, lest the wild beasts grow too numerous for you.*

So they knew the plan, they were to take over steadily as they advanced, little by little.

This is usually the case with a lot of the promises God makes to us. When He promises to bring us victory or prosperity he gives us the opportunity and expects us to take them. God puts you in an advantageous position and expects you to trust Him and take your opportunity

The Lord once said to me one early morning, '*rely on the structures of opportunity of God*'. I believe that many Christians suffer unnecessarily because we do not take advantage of the opportunities God brings our way.

We sometimes live as though Christ did not conquer the world on our behalf. He did. If you are a born again Christian and still suffering and allowing the enemy to oppress you, check again, it may be your fault.

The bible has told us in many places that Jesus died to set us free. He already died not that he will die if we believe. If Jesus sets you free you are free indeed (John 8:36)

Hebrew 2:14-15 tell us that

> *Since therefore the children share in flesh and blood, he himself likewise partook of the same nature, that through death he might destroy him who has the power of death, that is, the devil, and deliver all those who through fear of death were subject to lifelong bondage.*

If therefore, you still live in fear and bondage of the devil, it is not God's fault and it does not mean that Jesus did not die for you. You have to decide to walk and live in victory.

When God promised to bring Israel to the Promise Land, He did not promise to maintain the land for them. It was up to them to maintain their victory, or constantly call on God to help keep that victory. It would have been easier if they fully obeyed God's instruction to effectively occupy the land by driving out all the enemies in the territory.

If we proclaim that we are delivered and continue to court the devil and his agents they will become a threat to us and even deny us of fully enjoying the victory that Christ won for us through his death.

It is your duty to maintain your victory and by that declare the praise of God who has called you out of darkness into his own marvellous light. We can maintain our victory by constantly living the life of God; the life of righteousness.

5

Take Your Blessings.

How long will you wait before you begin to take possession of the land that the LORD, the God of your ancestors, has given you? (Joshua 18:3)

Many people desire a miracle from God but do not know how to present their need to Him and so do not see the manifestation of God's power. James tells us;

Ye ask, and receive not, because ye ask amiss... (James 4:3 KJV)

Prayer
Ask and it will be given to you; seek and you will find; knock and the door will be opened to you. (Matthew 7:7)

Prayer is essentially communicating with God. In prayer we meet God and God meets us. Just like you would to a loving father, or a dear friend, we present our needs to God when we come to him in prayer. Prayer is not a way to manipulate God into doing our will or going against His will. We should, however be bold and honest in our prayers.

Prayer can change any situation. That challenge before you which seem impossible can be turned around through prayer, no matter who has advised you concerning it and told you that it is impossible and that things cannot change. Jesus said that all things are possible to the one that believes (Mark 9:23). The prophet Isaiah brought words to Hezekiah when he was terminally ill and said;

> *This is what the LORD says: Put your house in order, because you are going to die; you will not recover.* (2 Kings 20:1)

This was a death sentence from the Lord through the prophet. This is worse than a doctor telling somebody they will die of any illness in a few days. This was a word from God Himself. But Hezekiah did not accept it; he decided to take his chance with

God. Since he was at least given some time, he took his opportunity and prayed to God. He turned his face to the wall and prayed. There was no other option; God's mercy and kindness was his only option. God heard him and cancelled the death sentence.

> *Go back and tell Hezekiah, the ruler of my people, 'This is what the LORD, the God of your father David, says: I have heard your prayer and seen your tears; I will heal you.* (2 Kings 20:5)

Hezekiah could have accepted death and prepared himself for it, but he did not. His simple honest prayer to God secured his healing and gave him another 15 years to live. You have nothing to lose if you pray. It is your key to unlocking your blessings. Pray, pray and pray.

As mentioned earlier, I believe there are four main aspects of prayer;

1. Asking in faith,
2. Listening for God's instructions
3. Obeying God's instructions

4. Receiving the miracle

You have to ask in faith. All things are possible to him that believes. Do not come to God as an option or alternative to other avenues of having your needs met. You must come to Him as the ONLY option and believing that He is able to grant your request. God will not share His glory with any other so you may not receive if you do not come to Him wholeheartedly.

Listen for God's instructions. Jesus taught us to watch and pray. So when you pray you must pay attention to any leading of the Holy Spirit. You are now a child of God and have the Spirit of God in you, this Spirit speaks and leads.

> *Whether you turn to the right or to the left, your ears will hear a voice behind you, saying, "This is the way; walk in it.* (Isaiah 30:21)

When you pay attention to the Holy Spirit, He may tell you what to do about a particular challenge or tell you when your prayer has been answered so that you can move to the next stage of ACTING in faith.

Obey God's instruction. Disobedience is one of the biggest stealers of our blessings. Another is pride. If the servants in John 2:1-10 did not draw from the jars they just filled with water and taken it to the master of ceremony as Jesus commanded, there probably will not be a miracle. Also if the Disciples waited to see the actual multiplication of the loaves and fish in John 6:1-13, more than five thousand people may not have been fed by that miracle.

You have prayed about something, you must act in accordance with God's word concerning that situation. Take the Step. God's word about our blessings may come through revelation to us or may already be contained in the written Word; the Bible. Study the bible and live according to it, that is the way to make your way prosperous and have good success (Joshua 1:8).

Receive your miracle. It will be a shame if you struggle against opposition to get a blessing or favour and may be, waited in a long queue for it and when it is your turn you walk away without taking the thing for which you have laboured. Receiving your miracle entails actions. You must act by either actually taking steps to receive what you have asked for in faith or you wait on God. Waiting on God does not mean a period of inactivity. It is a period of watchful patience. You are watching patiently to receive what you know He has already granted. While you are waiting you must declare your victory. You continually speak of receiving that favour from God. You are a child of God and your Father created the world by the 'Word of His power' (Hebrews 1:3), you too can create your world by what you say; 'open wide your mouth and I will fill it' (Psalm 81:10).

A man's belly shall be satisfied with the fruit of His mouth; and with the increase of his lips shall he be filled. Death and life are in the power of the tongue: and they that love it shall eat the fruit thereof. (Proverbs 18:20-21)

Keep declaring your victory and you will see it come to pass.

Fasting

Fasting is the abstinence from food and leisure in other to spend time with God and the things of the Spirit. It is a platform for supernatural release. Prayer and fasting which is done with understanding can release any miracle and unlock any closed destiny.

Jesus told the disciples, concerning the boy they could not heal, that;

> *This kind can come forth by nothing but by prayer and fasting* (Mark 9:29)

This tells us that some things will not move by prayer alone, but by prayer and fasting.

Many people, however, abstain from food but do not pray. They get busy doing their daily or routine jobs on the fasting days. This removes the power of a spiritual fast and makes it an ordinary physical exercise. The bible says in Isaiah 58 verse 3;

> *Wherefore have we fasted, say they, and thou seest not? wherefore have we afflicted our soul, and thou takest no knowledge? Behold, in the day of your fast ye find pleasure, and exact all your labours.* (Isaiah 58:3 KJV)

Abstaining from food without a quality time for prayer is not the kind of fasting which produces results.

In the same Isaiah 58:6-14, we read of the true fast recommended by the Lord Himself and the benefits of a true fast. Some of the blessings from a true fast include;

Verse 8;
1. *Your light will break forth as the morning.*
2. *Your health shall spring forth speedily.*
3. *Your righteousness will go before you.*
4. *God's glory will be your rear guard.*

Verse 9;
1. *You will call on the Lord and He will answer.*
2. *You will cry and He will say; Here I am.*

Verse 14; He will make you ride upon the high places of the earth.

There are many other blessings in that scripture – Isaiah 58:6-14

Word of God

There is more assurance that we will receive answers to our prayers if we pray the will of God. You may need a divine revelation to know God's particular will for your life, but the will of God for all His children can be clearly seen in the scriptures. Praying with the scriptures is praying the will of God. Therefore praying with the scriptures is a very effective way to pray because that way you pray the written Word of God into the creative Word; God does what He says or has said in the scripture.

If you are sick, for instance, pray with the scriptures that clearly promise your healing and God will heal you, there are many of them in the Bible. I remember one of my earliest experiences of divine healing. I had read the Book of Romans and came to chapter eight and verse eleven where it says;

And if the Spirit of him who raised Jesus from the dead is living in you, he who raised Christ from the dead will also give life to your mortal bodies because of his Spirit who lives in you. (Romans 8:11)

Knowing that I am a child of God and that God's Spirit lives in me I placed my hand on the spot where I felt pain and prayed quoting that scripture and the pain stopped instantly and I was healed. This was my very first experience and I have seen many more since then. I did not engage in a long prayer. The knowledge of that scripture made my prayer brief and opened that door of blessing.

When you pray with the scriptures you are saying that you believe the words and in the power of Him who spoke the words, to do what He has said He will do. This faith can heal any disease, unlock the doors to any challenge and deliver any delayed blessing to you.

Read the bible always and through the power of the Holy Spirit you will understand the will of God concerning your life and the challenges that may arise, then pray with the scripture that concern your needs.

After you have prayed
There may be something you have been asking God to give you, or a prophecy that was made about your life, and you have been waiting for its manifestation, it is time for you to look carefully around you to see if the promise has even been brought within your reach but you have not yet taken it.

You may now be in your very own promise land without knowing it. May be all you need now is to possess your possession; to drive out the already defeated enemy. A friend once told me of how, as a child, he went to gather firewood from a nearby bush and while looking for dry wood he saw a snake, the type that they ate in that part of the world, and instinctively he ran after it and just as the snake tried to run into a hole in the ground he grabbed it by the tail, pulled it out of the hole, swung it round and hit it on the ground. He hit so hard that the snake laid there motionless. Then all of a sudden it dawned on him that this was really a snake and he ran off too afraid to pick it up. I do not fully remember now how the story ended, but I think he then called on his mother to come and take the kill. He had killed the snake without thinking of it but now it was dead he is too afraid to have the honour of bringing home his kill.

Many Christians labour hard to get a blessing; they fast and pray and believe, and then suddenly fear sets in and they begin to analyse and magnify the situation until it appears bigger than God in their eyes and then they give up.

God can defeat your enemy and inflict them with fear of you, but you must drive them out. God will not force His blessing on you; you have to take it.

Rely On God's Opportunities

Look around at the opportunities around you to be sure the devil is not holding you in bondage and denying you God's blessings. You could be like the person who is living in abject poverty because he did not know he had an abundant inheritance.

Prayerfully consider the circumstances around you. It may be that you are already in your 'promise land' but living like a servant or slave in it.

Arise child of God and take the kingdom! Possess your possession. It is up to you to drive out the enemy and enjoy your blessing. The Lord has given you authority to do that. Stop being nice and polite to the devil and his bondage, he is wicked and does not care about you. If the devil has his way he will destroy you first.

Jesus said;

> *Behold, I have given you authority to tread upon serpents and scorpions and over all the power of the enemy; and nothing shall hurt you.* (Luke 10:19).

Take your authority and overpower him first. If you leave the enemy in your territory he will become a snare to you.

The enemy may be lurking around but they are already defeated. If you are a child of God then you are a victor, so live like one.

> *For whatever is born of God overcomes the world; and this is the victory that overcomes the world, our faith* (1 John 5:4).

I know for sure that God fulfils His promise. It may delay but it will come to pass.

Discern and Wait on Him.

It may also be the case that the Lord is keeping your promise for an appointed time. He makes all things beautiful in His time (Ecclesiastes 3:11). God never lies; He has no need for it. He does not try to impress and has no need to impress anyone.

Sometimes God's promises may take time in coming, and people may begin to doubt that they will come to pass. In the example of our father Abraham, it took twenty-five years before the fulfilment of the promised child, Isaac. The Lord told Habakkuk;

> *For still the vision awaits its time; it hastens to the end — it will not lie. If it seem slow, wait for it; it will surely come, it will not delay.* (Habakkuk 2:2-3)

Do not continue life as usual after reading this book. Pray to God to open your eyes so that you can see where you are in His plans and if you are not where you should be then you have to make a move.

Read God's instruction to Joshua and prayerfully apply it to challenges you face and this may be the beginning of the change you desire in your life.

> *After the death of Moses the servant of the LORD, the LORD said to Joshua the son of Nun, Moses' minister, "Moses my servant is dead; now therefore arise, go over this Jordan,*

you and all this people, into the land which I am giving to them, to the people of Israel. Every place that the sole of your foot will tread upon I have given to you, as I promised to Moses. (Joshua 1:1-3)

He continued;

No man shall be able to stand before you all the days of your life; as I was with Moses, so I will be with you; I will not fail you or forsake you. Be strong and of good courage; for you shall cause this people to inherit the land which I swore to their fathers to give them. Only be strong and very courageous, being careful to do according to all the law which Moses my servant commanded you; turn not from it to the right hand or to the left, that you may have good success wherever you go. (Joshua 1:5-7)

It is time to make that move. God told Joshua; *'only be strong and very courageous'.* Boldness and courage is a sign that you believe God has power to do what he says He will do. Make that bold move. Enter your promised inheritance. Take the kingdom.

When you receive that blessing remember to testify to the glory of God in other to encourage your fellow believers and preserve your victory.

www.ingramcontent.com/pod-product-compliance
Lightning Source LLC
Chambersburg PA
CBHW031429040426
42444CB00006B/755